SATISFIED

This book was made possible by the generosity and trust of my father Ian Kocho and my husband John Douglas

Thanks to Tom, Libby, Lynn, Gordon, Joan, Ruth, Peter, Kathy, Kathryn & Ellen

'God is our refuge and strength' - Ps46

Copyright 2023 by Judy I.K (Iris Kocho) Douglas

Illustration: Vanessa Bong - vessillustration.com
Design: Matthew Brown - takodesign.studio
Edited by Jo Stockdale

Young Adult Non Fiction/ Religious / Christian / General, Dating, Family & Relationships
Religion / Christian Living / General, Family & Relationships. Love & Marriage
Religion / Christian Ministry / Youth
Religion / Sexuality & Gender Studies

Unless otherwise noted, Scripture quotations are taken from Holy Bible, New International Version® Anglicized, NIV® Copyright © 1979, 1984, 2011 by Biblica, Inc.® Used by permission. All rights reserved worldwide; Scripture quotations marked the message are taken from THE MESSAGE. Copyright © by Eugene H. Peterson 1993, 2002. Used by permission of Tyndale House Publishers, Inc; Scripture quotations marked gnt are taken from the Good News Translation in Today's English Version—Second Edition. Copyright © 1992 by American Bible Society. Used by permission; Scripture quotations marked ICB are taken from The Holy Bible, International Children's Bible® Copyright© 1986, 1988, 1999, 2015 by Thomas Nelson. Used by permission; Scripture quotations marked NRSV are taken from the New Revised Standard Version Bible, copyright 1989, Division of Christian Education of the National Council of the Churches of Christ in the United States of America. Used by permission. All rights reserved.

Paperback ISBN: 978-0-6456357-0-6
E-book ISBN: 978-0-6456357-1-3

Introduction
1. You are Loved
2. Body Balance
3. The Book in the Middle
4. Swimming
5. Cake
6. Powerful
7. Verb
8. Controller
9. Entrée or Main?
10. The Sex Myth
11. Monk Life
12. Single-minded
13. Satisfied
14. The Love Tank
15. Judge Not
16. Solo
17. Spectator Sport
18. TJ Says
19. Same-Sex Sex
20. More to Say
21. Pink-boy, Blue-girl
22. Comfort and Balance
23. Alterations
24. Consumer or Covenant?
25. Following
26. A Last Word
Read, Listen, Watch
Notes

'There's an elephant in the room.' It's a phrase people use when something is huge and obvious but everyone's acting like it's not there.

This book is about 'the elephant in the room'. Sex is everywhere and most of us are thinking about it – so let's talk more. Not just the crass or jokey way we talk with our friends and not just the formal, clinical information we get In Sex Ed class. If we are going to figure out what's best for our sex lives, and what will really help us find a good life; we need something with more meaning. Join me as we look in the pages of the Bible and discover the stories of followers of Jesus. God's wisdom can actually help us in our thinking and life choices about sex and relationships. We can be satisfied.

'I'M ABSOLUTELY CONVINCED THAT NOTHING—NOTHING LIVING OR DEAD, ANGELIC OR DEMONIC, TODAY OR TOMORROW, HIGH OR LOW, THINKABLE OR UNTHINKABLE—ABSOLUTELY NOTHING CAN GET BETWEEN US AND GOD'S LOVE BECAUSE OF THE WAY THAT JESUS OUR MASTER HAS EMBRACED US.'[1]

YOU ARE LOVED

When it comes to sex, maybe you feel proud because you're obeying all the rules you think you should. You might have your own ideas about sex and are ready for a fight, ready to challenge anyone who disagrees with you. You could be feeling sad or bad because of memories; experiences you didn't like or didn't have any choice about. Maybe you have regrets about choices you made, or you might feel guilty because you have used or hurt someone. Maybe you have no experience with sex at all but would really like to one day.

Maybe, like a lot of people, it's all just too embarrassing to talk about. Whatever you are feeling, please remember:

YOU ARE LOVED

You are loved. The most powerful being in the universe – God – has known you and loved you since before you were born. You are not an accident, you are not a mistake. You are valuable.

When it comes to sex, the best place to be is close to God and His love. Believe it or not, you can talk to God about everything to do with sex. God is super wise and knows it all already anyway.

You were not meant to be alone working sex out for yourself. God wants what is best for you. God knows you completely, God likes you, God wants to hang out with you and show you His wisdom and truth. Working out our lives in relation to sex is part of the great journey of life. For Christians, it's an important part of the journey of faith.

BODY BALANCE

There is no such thing as a perfect body. Human bodies can be big, small, muscular, slight, hairy, smooth, angular or round, and all different colours. There are differences in how our bodies look and move; sometimes the differences bring extra challenges to the user.

There is much more to a human body than what you might see on an advertising billboard or an Instagram photo. Everyday bodies don't look like billboard bodies. They are much more interesting.

For a start they are in 3D not 2D. They are also warm not cold, and real not fake. Real people with real bodies have feelings, thoughts and ideas, they can actually really love you and be loved in return. Reality is much more fun! Don't ever expect a real person to look like a fake flat photo.

With all your bumps, bits, bones and blemishes, your body is beautiful. Even with its imperfections, your body is an amazing, functioning marvel. God designs incredible things, you included!

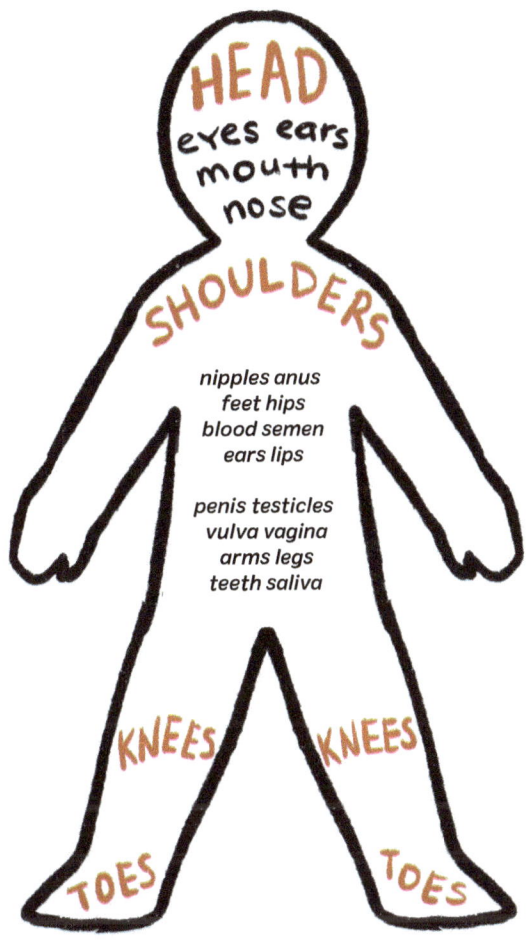

'For you created my inmost being; you knit me together in my mother's womb.
I praise you because I am fearfully and wonderfully made; your works are wonderful, I know that full well.'[2]

'God created humankind in his own image, in the image of God he created them; male and female he created them... God saw everything that he had made, and indeed, it was VERY GOOD...'[3]

'But in fact God has placed the parts in the body, every one of them, just as he wanted them to be.'[4]

'And even the very hairs of your head are all numbered.'[5]

As you grow into your teens your body changes. You get bigger and hairier. The soft, fleshy, sexual parts of our bodies grow and change too. You might get a monthly period or an unexpected erection. Some people don't mind all this happening and some of us find the changes difficult. God sees and knows about all the changes in your body as well as all our deepest and craziest thoughts and feelings. God is a great listener, you can tell Him everything. You might even hear a wise whisper back if you take the time to listen.

Sexual feelings, looking for beauty and hoping for pleasure are part of who you are. These feelings are a natural and normal part of life. They are yours to enjoy. At times these feelings can be overwhelming or hard to control. As you grow there will be times when you need strength and logic to stay in a healthy and balanced place.

It can be hard to find the words, but if you have worries about your body, or anything to do with sex, talk to wiser, older, trustworthy people. It can be embarrassing to open up, but it can really help.

THE BOOK IN THE MIDDLE

In the middle of the Bible is a little book with big ideas about sex. The poems of the Song of Songs are sensual, physical, dreamy and erotic. They are also quite funny to read out loud.

'Let him kiss me with the kisses of his mouth – for your love is more delightful than wine… Take me away with you – let us hurry! Let the king bring me into his chambers.'

'My beloved is to me a sachet of myrrh resting between my breasts… How beautiful you are, my darling! Oh, how beautiful! Your eyes are doves. How handsome you are, my beloved! Oh, how charming! And our bed is verdant.'

'Your lips drop sweetness as the honeycomb, my bride; milk and honey are under your tongue.'

'I found the one my heart loves. I held him and would not let him go.'

'Let my beloved come into his garden and taste its choice fruits. I have come into my garden, my sister, my bride; I have gathered my myrrh with my spice. I have eaten my honeycomb and my honey; I have drunk my wine and my milk. Eat, friends, and drink; drink your fill of love.'

'I would give you spiced wine to drink, the nectar of my pomegranates. His left arm is under my head and his right arm embraces me.' [6]

The people in these poems think and dream about having sex, they are overcome and amazed by beauty. They also get frustrated when things get complicated by family and friends. It's joyful as well as risky.[7]

Sex is a very good thing. It was God's idea in the first place; God made us with all our sexual feelings. It is an amazing world of physical and emotional experience. Sex has a strong, magnetic pull and attraction. It's a part of life to be enjoyed and celebrated.

The Song of Songs also says:

'Love is strong as death, passion fierce as the grave. Its flashes are flashes of fire, a raging flame. Many waters cannot quench love, neither can floods drown it.' [8]

The drive and energy of sex can feel overwhelming. It can distract us, fill all our brain space and drown out logic or any other thoughts. That is probably why the Song of Songs also has a chorus that runs through the book:

'Do not arouse or awaken love until it so desires.' [9]

The woman in Song of Songs keeps telling her girlfriends, 'Do not arouse or awaken love until it so desires'. She worries that her younger friends will 'enter such an intense and risky relationship too quickly. Love is hard work and risky. They need to wait for the right time and the right person'. [10]

For followers of Jesus, sex is just for a particular time and place in life. The lovers in Song of Songs, a man and a woman, are celebrating the power and joy of sex as they begin and share a life together as husband and wife.

SWIMMING

A long luxurious swim on a hot day. There's nothing like it. Lake, ocean or river, the more natural and pristine the better. Watery places have amazing potential for enjoyment and pleasure. Swimming is a beautiful sensual experience, but it also has its dangers.

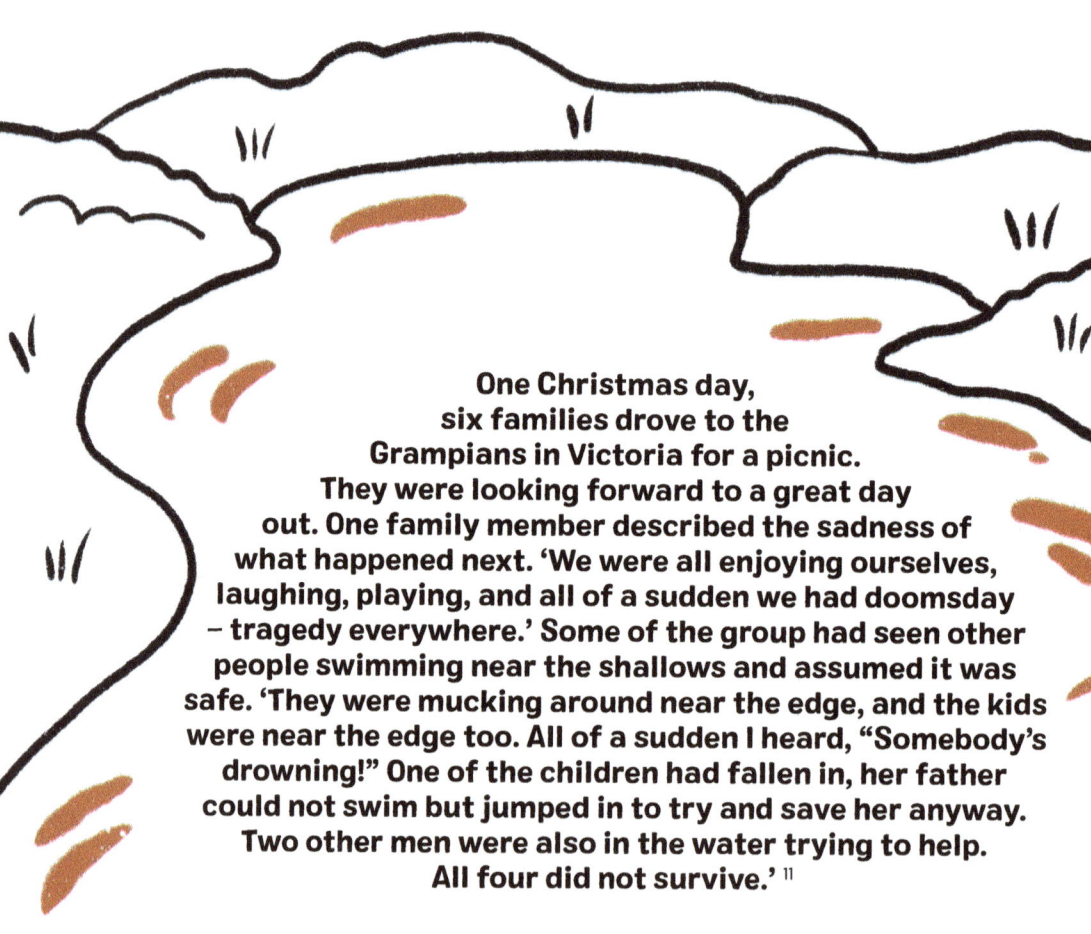

One Christmas day, six families drove to the Grampians in Victoria for a picnic. They were looking forward to a great day out. One family member described the sadness of what happened next. 'We were all enjoying ourselves, laughing, playing, and all of a sudden we had doomsday – tragedy everywhere.' Some of the group had seen other people swimming near the shallows and assumed it was safe. 'They were mucking around near the edge, and the kids were near the edge too. All of a sudden I heard, "Somebody's drowning!" One of the children had fallen in, her father could not swim but jumped in to try and save her anyway. Two other men were also in the water trying to help. All four did not survive.' [11]

In Australia, there's a huge bunch of rules and regulations around our beloved swimming activity. We have flags to swim between, lifesavers, learn to swim courses, shark nets, shark alarms, pool rules, lap lane indicators, depth signs, flotation devices, sunscreen, rashies, instructions on avoiding crocodiles and jellyfish. None of these things are meant to kill our enjoyment of the sensual pleasure of swimming.

RULES AND REGULATIONS KEEP PEOPLE SAFE FROM THE DANGERS AND ENHANCE THE ENJOYMENT.

The Bible celebrates sex in Song of Songs, but it also has useful things to say about limits and rules when it comes to sex and relationships. For our safety, sex needs guidelines.

'In the original creation, God made male and female to be together. Because of this, a man leaves father and mother, and in marriage he becomes one flesh with a woman—no longer two individuals, but forming a new unity. Because God created this organic union of the two sexes, no one should desecrate his art by cutting them apart.' [12]

'There's more to sex than mere skin on skin. Sex is as much spiritual mystery as physical fact. As written in Scripture, "The two become one." Since we want to become spiritually one with the Master, we must not pursue the kind of sex that avoids commitment and intimacy, leaving us more lonely than ever—the kind of sex that can never "become one."' [13]

CAKE

SEX IS LIKE THE ICING ON A HOMEMADE BIRTHDAY CAKE.

A bowl of icing is not meant to be eaten on its own. A homemade birthday cake is produced by someone who cares. They take time and effort to gather the ingredients, follow a recipe, mix and bake the cake. Just when they think it's done, there is more waiting while the cake cools. The icing goes on the cake at the end of a long process. A process of loving kindness.

Sex for followers of Jesus is a package deal. The icing is meant to be eaten with the cake. The Bible's Song of Songs describes how sexual desire and passion are held together with long-term love and commitment that includes family, community and being together in the whole of life (even the boring bits).

This cake has so many amazing layers: friendship, fun, attraction, doing life together, growing trust, time, being together with friends, growing a family, church, practical life choices, gifts, kind and encouraging words, maturity, listening, hugs and kisses, prayer, common interests, commitment.

In the 2020s, it might be out of fashion, and it might not be what most people do, but it is still an awesome thing to keep sex for the time when you can stand before your friends and family and make a public commitment to lifelong faithfulness.

In a world where there are many bad and untrustworthy people, this big public promise shows integrity, honesty and character. Human beings don't always live up to their promises, but having sex with someone, knowing that they have made that heartfelt, serious promise to you, definitely makes it easier to trust, be vulnerable and maybe even be okay with them seeing you naked. Keeping sex for after the celebration of marriage is still a really good idea. It's our wise God's good idea.

And please don't forget: being married is more than one special day. There's a heartfelt intention at the beginning but it's followed up by an everyday, lifelong commitment shown in practical actions and words. Even though things can fall apart, this is still an impressive life goal worth working towards.

'I will never forget that moment, standing there in front of all our family and friends, when he looked me straight in the eye and said, "With all that I am, and all that I have, I honour YOU". My eyes welled with joyful tears. That night, after a great big party, we had sex for the very first time. I have never felt so alive, but I also felt cradled in the safe place of a life we would now share together. I didn't have to guess or hope for what might be. Our lives had knotted together over time and our clear intentions had been spoken aloud to each other in God's holy presence.' [14]

In Jonathan Franzen's novel Purity there is a young woman called Pip Tyler. Through the book she has a number of super intense, confronting and disappointing experiences with sex. She finds this all depressing and disappointing, her heart gets damaged and grows cold. Along the way she meets Jason and they start playing tennis, no sex, just tennis. They end up playing a lot of tennis, months and months of just connecting over the net in the simple joy of a game. She finds her heart coming alive again and lasting love eventually blooms. [15]

'As a kid, going through my parents' experiences of sex and relationships really impacted me. I grew up in a complicated family: my parents broke up when I was ten as my dad left my mum for my now step-mum; I have a half-sister and a step-brother. I am so very thankful that my wife and I both follow Jesus and chose to keep sex until we were married. We struggled, and it wasn't easy to wait, but now we share something together that no one else has ever been a part of. We have been married for four years, and together with God, my beautiful wife and I are on a different pathway of marriage and sex. I think our kids have a much better chance of growing up without the problems and baggage I had.' [16]

POWERFUL

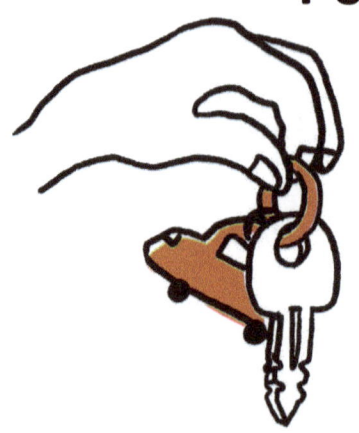

'So you've never driven a car? Not a problem, have my keys, jump in and figure it out as you go. You'll be fine.'

Cars are powerful. They are useful for getting you to places, but they are complex machines, with the capability to go extremely fast. Without knowledge, careful guidance and road rules, these powerful machines can damage or even kill the driver, the passengers and anyone else who happens to be in the general area.

Sex is an awesome gift but it's so important to take time to learn, get guidance;

UNDERSTAND THE POWER.

Like glue, the close intimacy of being naked with another person and the intense pleasure of orgasm is a biological process that creates feelings of intense connection and love. Females are more likely to experience this.

For males, the process can be different. Having sex and experiencing orgasm casually or early in a relationship can short circuit the build-up of the feelings that increase the desire for long-term love and commitment.

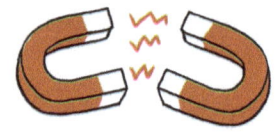

These biological processes were designed by God to create bonding and help two very different humans 'stick together for the long-haul' of life. [17]
Without understanding the power of sex we can use it casually and too quickly. We can miss out on the deeper experience that sex was meant to be, miss out on finding and keeping the lifelong love we all desire. [18]

It is so important to remember that in the natural way, by God's design, sex makes babies. Even in the modern world, with access to many forms of contraception, sex still puts you in a place where becoming a parent is a possibility. Sex is connected to responsibility. It's part of the joy and complex grown-up, lifelong commitment of raising children.

*'SEX IS NOT JUST ABOUT BODIES.
IT TOUCHES OUR SOULS.'*

SEX HAS A DARK SIDE

The experience of sex creates lasting memories that shape our lives. When people have had to endure unwanted sex or abuse, when you are powerless to make it stop, it's hard to just forget. **This kind of history can hurt**. It can keep on affecting people's thinking and actions for a long time.

We know that children were not meant to have sex; when **sex abuse** *happens it can bring deep confusion and sadness.* **It damages**.

Sex doesn't stop having a deep effect just because you've reached a birthday and are legally allowed. Even when sex is a good experience, fun and playful, it sets off **powerful thoughts and intense emotions**. You may not think that this will happen to you, but there will be break ups. When people have shared the deep intimacy of sex it can bring **long-lasting emotional pain**; it makes the break-up rejection feel so much worse.

Sex was meant for lasting, joyful connection, but relationships go sour. It's tragic that people who have shared the close physical experience of sex can then hate each other or be **strangers again, embarrassed and ashamed**.

And what happens when people say yes to having sex but for different reasons? One person is looking for a casual good time, while the other is secretly hoping that sex will help their loneliness and the loving connection will last.

God meant sex to create joy but it can bring hurt, disappointment and broken dreams to people looking for real love.

You could also get a chronic illness through a **sexually transmitted disease**. What's worse, you could give someone else a serious disease.
Sex has physical effects and long-term, life-changing consequences.

'THE PAIN OF PATIENCE IS FAR LESS THAN THE PAIN OF REGRET.'

Love is a small word that means so many different things. When someone says 'I love you' they might just be describing feelings. They might be saying they feel deeply connected or physically attracted to you; you probably make their heart warm and mushy. When used this way, love is an adjective, it describes feelings. But ...

LOVE IS A VERB

Love is a lot more than feelings. It is a long list of good actions that feelings of love can produce.

Love can even exist without feelings. *When Jesus asked His followers to love their enemies, He didn't mean He wanted them to have warm or mushy feelings for them. Remember, love is a verb. Jesus was describing actions. He followed up by describing what He really meant: 'Do good to those who hate you.'* [19]

Generally, we are not so great at this kind of love. God is so different. God specialises in the verb kind of love.

Loving feelings come and go, but when love is an action, a verb, it keeps the doing going. It goes on loving even when there are no nice feelings; even when people don't deserve it, when they aren't being loving; even when people look like an enemy. That's how God loves and that is what true love looks like.

The popular writer John Green describes the confusion about what the word 'love' means.

'The word "love" is an unmitigated disaster. I mean, I love reading detective novels, and I also love my children, and yet the feeling of reading a detective novel has almost no kinship with the feeling of building Lego with my kids. I love my friends, but not like I love my wife. There are so many loves, and only just the one word in English... But when we talk about love at first sight, of course, we're almost always talking about romantic love and the near-immediate attraction humans sometimes experience. Indeed, studies have shown that people make conclusions about attractiveness almost instantaneously—in less than a second. But attraction isn't love... I think the mistake is when we conflate the kind of love that makes us fail exams with the kind of love that can share the great upheavals of the human life. The one is a fever or a fall; The other sees you through fevers and falls.' [20]

ARE YOU READY FOR THE CHALLENGE OF REAL LOVE?

The actions of love

Love is patient. Love is kind.

It cares more for others than for self.

Love isn't envious.

It doesn't want what it doesn't have.

Love doesn't have a swelled head.

Love doesn't force itself on others,

It isn't always 'me first'.

Love doesn't fly off the handle.

It doesn't keep score of mistakes and wrongs.

It doesn't revel when others grovel.

Love takes pleasure in honesty and truth.

Love always looks for the best.

It doesn't look back to past failures

But keeps going to the end. [21]

'What we got is real love, it ain't a big deal love. But it has its appeal, it's real, it's here, it's love... It's not into kisses, it ain't getting your wishes, it's doing the dishes, that's real, real love.' [22]

CONTROLLER

Humans' desire for sex is triggered in loads of different ways. A particular person, a situation, certain words, particular clothing, images, great-looking body parts and all kinds of other things can spark people up and fill our bodies and thoughts with those passionate sexual feelings. Human beings are very varied when it comes to sex. Some people are not that interested, they would be happy with a hug or a good conversation. Some people have a very strong sex drive. People are an infinite variety. There is no one normal.

When it comes to sexual feelings and desire, you have the controller. Healthy self-control will mean you can avoid a lot of big problems in life. Just doing what your body wants can damage relationships, seriously hurt others or even get you in trouble with the law. We can learn to use our brains to control our bodies.

That powerful feeling of wanting sex. You need it NOW! It can feel like nothing else in the world matters. It's so INTENSE.

- *These strong, craving feelings are normal. They are part of how God made you to be. Try not to bury the feeling, be honest with yourself.*

- *Find a healthy way to release the physical pressure. Go for a run, play sport, jump in the pool or play some loud music.*

- *Activate your brain, have a think and a pray. You can be honest with God about all your thoughts and feelings. You are in a tricky place, but remember you are loved.*

Jesus is our living example. Jesus had power and control but He chose never to use His power to get things for Himself. Jesus gave up all His power, His whole life, so that we could find meaning and life. He is the Son of God, who loved you and gave Himself for you.

> *'When you do things, do not let selfishness or pride be your guide. Be humble and give more honor to others than to yourselves. Do not be interested only in your own life, but be interested in the lives of others.'* [23]

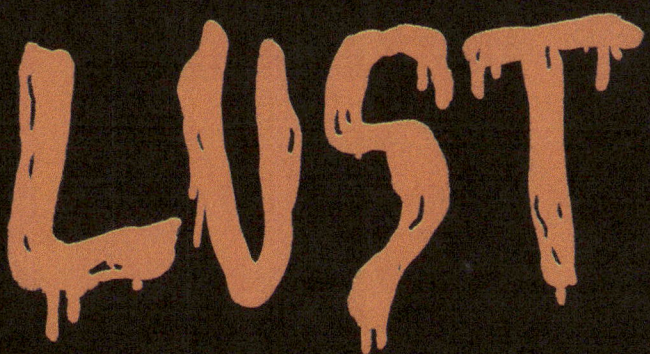

Lust is when normal, healthy and natural sexual feelings get twisted to the dark side.

Lust is about getting **what I want for me** and not caring about the other person and what is best for them. Instead of self-control, lust is only interested in taking. It tries to **steal or control others to get what it wants**. God wants us to avoid lust and not use people just for our own sexual pleasure.

Keep sex as the beautiful and holy thing God intended it to be. Sex was never intended to be risky or guilt-ridden. [24]

EIGHT BAD REASONS TO HAVE SEX

- You have the opportunity.
- You want to prove you can.
- You don't want to look childish or weak.
- You want to show you are attractive or lovable.
- You want to rebel.
- Drugs or alcohol are weakening your logic.
- Someone is telling you they need sex to keep the relationship going.
- You want to claim someone for yourself.

There is a chance you are reading this and you have been hurt by someone's lust. Maybe you've had unwanted or hurtful experiences with sex that have left you feeling sad, lonely or confused. Please remember you are loved and valuable no matter what. Whatever you are feeling now, the future can be better. It's hard to find the words but it helps to talk. It might be with your parents or someone else mature and wise, but share your story. Things can really change when we talk things out and get support.

Maybe *you* have already hurt someone through lust. We all make mistakes and wrong choices and it's important to be honest and admit that it's seriously wrong to hurt others; but you are not doomed. When we have messed up and done selfish things, we can say sorry, we can try and make things right. God forgives us and always loves us. God also gives us spiritual strength. We can ask Him for the strength we need to avoid lust and choose real love.

ENTRÉE OR MAIN?

SEX IS LIKE THE MAIN COURSE OF A GOURMET MEAL.

Gourmet meals usually have lots of things to eat and drink before you get to the main course. It's the same with sex. Long before the main course there are entrées, like having long talks, sharing fun activities together, staring into each other's eyes, holding hands, hugs and kisses. People might go further: talk about sex with each other, have longer cuddles, touch each other's sensitive sexual parts, be naked with each other and experience growing intensity in pleasurable sexual feelings. What's helpful and what should we leave till later?

It's really important not to rush. Enjoy this in-between time. There's a whole world for friendship and maybe a few kisses and embraces to enjoy. When you are younger, it's best to avoid too much intensity leading up to sex.

The main course of sex is the closest you can physically be to another person when you are fully naked. There's no turning back. Two bodies become one, the intense feelings form a strong bond. God has reserved this amazing activity for responsible people who have committed their lives to each other and are ready for the possibility of becoming parents.

Different Christian groups and cultures have different ideas and rules about what is physically appropriate before the lifelong commitment of marriage. Some have strict rules, like not even being alone together or kissing before getting engaged. Others might say kissing and cuddles are part of normal teenage romantic relationships. School sex education might just say that everything is fine as long as you are safe from pregnancy and disease.

Remember God and talk to Him about your romantic relationships. God knows about everything going on in your life already, you don't have to hide from Him. God is with us and wants what is best for us.

As you get older, the length and quality of your relationship is an important factor when deciding what is best. What you might share physically when you have known someone a long time and there is trust and hope for a life together is different from when you have only just met someone or are testing out your relationship through going out together or dating. [25]

It's important to keep sexual feelings and desires alive. They are natural and normal. Instead of trying to bury your feelings, it's better to accept them as part of who you are. Acknowledge those passionate flames within you as something good in the right time and place.

Aim to keep sex as the beautiful and holy thing it was intended to be. If you start to feel uncomfortable or guilty, if the strength of feeling is stressful or overwhelming, or if you are having trouble staying in control, it's best to take a few steps back. **Self-control is a life skill we all need to practise.** It brings good things into our lives. [26]

If you are in a relationship waiting for marriage, **keep talking with each other and work out some helpful limits that are meaningful to you both.** Some people choose to go home to their own bed rather than stay over. They might choose to spend time with friends and family and in other activities that they really enjoy. God's way is so amazing that the longing, anticipation and waiting might make that future moment of coming together even more beautiful and incredible.

Australian journalist Rachel Hills interviewed more than two hundred people about their sex lives and then recorded her findings. [27]

Rachel uncovered a powerful, controlling idea in our popular culture:

The Sex Myth says that sex is 'more special, more significant, a source of greater thrills and more perfect pleasure than any other activity that humans engage in'. It's 'the idea that in sex we will find our truth'. [28]

We are now in 'a culture that tells us we must be sexy, sexually active and skilled in bed in order to be adequate human beings'. It 'teaches us that the truth of who we are can be found in our sex lives'. [29]

It seems that for many people now, sex has become THE most important thing, THE way to make meaning, THE source of identity and purpose in life.

So many songs we hear can make us think that sex and that special someone is the ultimate goal in life.

'You get me closer to God' [30]

*'She tells me, "Worship in the bedroom".
The only heaven I'll be sent to is when I'm alone with you'* [31]

'When I'm lost I just look in your eyes, you show me the meaning of life' [32]

YOU ARE SO MUCH MORE THAN WHAT YOU ARE SEXUALLY ATTRACTED TO.

Your value has nothing to do with having an active sex life or a life partner. Having sex does not make you more of anything, it does not give you an identity. Having sex is a part of life that some people get to enjoy but it's not the essential ingredient for happiness in life. It is not necessary for a full, valuable and interesting life.

Sex and romantic relationships are NOT the ultimate meaning and purpose of life.

We were made for something far greater. No person in this world, not even the one we desire and long for most, can satisfy fully or give us ultimate meaning.

Humans are designed with the need for a greater connection. A connection to God, the Power who made this whole world in more detail than a million Minecraft universes. This holy designer, the author, is The One where we find all truth, wisdom, goodness, beauty, purpose, strength and joy.

'We are half-hearted creatures fooling about with drink and sex and ambition when infinite joy is offered us, like an ignorant child who wants to go on making mud pies in a slum because he cannot imagine what is meant by the offer of a holiday at the sea. We are far too easily pleased.' [33]

MONK LIFE

There once lived a rich young man who lived a wild life. He had loads of sex and parties. He had money to get anything he liked. But it was not enough. He felt empty. This young man discovered a connection to God that satisfied his life more deeply than all the pleasures he had. **He sold all his possessions and lived his life single, without sex. He gave his life totally to work for God.** We know him today as **Saint Francis of Assisi.**

Francis learned to show God's love and wisdom in words but more importantly in actions. He was called on by world leaders to be a peacemaker in times of war. Francis was also passionate about caring for nature. He loved animals and plants and felt close to God in the wild outdoors. He brought many single people together to live in community. Together they tried to live as true followers of Jesus. Francis and his followers had a worldwide impact, and years and years later his words and life are remembered. Saint Francis is just one of many single people through the ages who has given mountains of their time and energy to change people's lives for good.

ROMANTIC RELATIONSHIPS AND MARRIAGE ARE FINE, BUT THEY ARE NOT WHAT IS MOST IMPORTANT FOR CHRISTIANS.

Single people have time and space to connect, care and share life with many people rather than just one main person. Everyone starts out single. Some move on, but some embrace singleness for life. Time on your own is a great time to grow. It's time to get to know God with less distractions and have adventures with more freedom.

Living single without sex does not have to be lonely or sad. It's definitely not unhealthy or bad or weird. Jesus was single! Jesus had close male and female friends and they shared in God's true love together. [34]

Jesus' life shows that you don't need sex to have the deepest and most meaningful, heart-filling relationships.

Being married, committed to someone for life, will bring joy as well as times of frustration, pain and suffering. Being single, free to serve God, will bring joy as well as times of frustration, pain and suffering.

Paul was a friend of Jesus. He was single too. Here's his advice to young Christians:

'Sometimes I wish everyone were single like me—a simpler life in many ways! But celibacy is not for everyone any more than marriage is. God gives the gift of the single life to some, the gift of the married life to others.' [35]

'I would like you to be free from concern. An unmarried man is concerned about the Lord's affairs – how he can please the Lord. But a married man is concerned about the affairs of this world – how he can please his wife – and his interests are divided. An unmarried woman or virgin is concerned about the Lord's affairs: her aim is to be devoted to the Lord in both body and spirit. But a married woman is concerned about the affairs of this world – how she can please her husband. I am saying this for your own good, not to restrict you, but that you may live in a right way in undivided devotion to the Lord.' [36]

SINGLE-MINDED

'Marriage is definitely not the promised land... We know that just because a couple have married, they are not necessarily either sexual or spiritual superstars. Many single people will know that their singleness often avails them of the time to work on increasingly deeper levels of personal spirituality, while married people have become distracted by sex, setting up homes or raising children... Many single people will also know that their wedded friends can be miserable in marriage... nothing is guaranteed by any means.' [37]

'A trailer at the cinema has been designed to make you want to enjoy the film it advertises. It gives you a foretaste of the future reality that could be yours if you watch the film. Sex and marriage have been designed to make you want to enjoy the future they advertise. They give you a foretaste of a future reality that could be yours if you follow Jesus. Any joy in sex and marriage now is just a trailer for the future joy all Christians will experience when they are united to God's Son Jesus forever. So, if you get to enjoy sex and marriage now you're just enjoying the trailer. If you don't enjoy sex and marriage now you are just missing the trailer. All who follow Jesus will get to enjoy the real thing.' [38]

'I believe in singleness. I see perfection in the exploding, love-drenched lives of single men and women. They lack no worldly thing. They do not need the validation of a sexual partner to be qualified in love. Our experiences are different but our calling is the same.' [39]

"[One] morning, unburdened and untethered, I realised I didn't need to have sex anymore… I was confused. Sex, previously my only language of love, wasn't deemed necessary in God's version of a life fully lived. In fact, it could apparently be used as a weapon of destruction in the wrong context. I had always figured that sex was part of the first conversation in figuring out if I would work with another person.

We were just bodies, touching, experimenting with chemistry. I didn't feel any need to wait for a magical number of dates. I had figured the natural spiritual process of sex and sexuality would uncover for me what my true feelings for that person were. But I found that, after the initial addictive hit, it just obscured them.

I had been searching for love in vain. I had tried on so many different shells, cowed under different bodies, and yet nothing felt like it could hold me it. I had acted on cravings and then realised I was never hungry.

As I held my body in that morning light, I found myself whispering a new apology and a new promise.

You don't have to do it anymore… You don't have to do anything you don't want to. You don't have to have sex.

A prison had been quietly unlocked with those words, and now I saw the door wide open. I was free. I didn't have to have sex to attract, impress or keep a partner. It wasn't required. I had nothing to prove.

Be it with men, women, one person or three – the issue of my spiritual, physical and creative worth was not ever going to be solved by sex. I was enough without sex. I was allowed to be alone in my body…

I held God now. I was not my own. I had been bought at a price.'" [40]

SATISFIED

When I was sixteen, I had these Bible verses on the back of my bedroom door: [41]

I really wanted to follow God and these words from the Bible were a great reminder that God understood all my passion for life and that I could trust Him for wherever life might lead. Here was a real promise that I would not be empty but full and satisfied; a constant reminder that my identity and worth were not in being physically attractive, having a special someone, a sex life, a life partner or children.

I can truly say I'm glad those words were there every day on the back of my door, reminding me to believe, reminding me to trust, reminding me where true happiness is. Sex is temporary, it's not a cure for the real spiritual hunger that is the source of our desires.

> **'Jesus said that if I thirst, I should come to Him.
> No one else can satisfy. I should come to Him.'** [42]

Jesus says:

**'Anyone who drinks the water I give will never thirst—not ever.
The water I give will be an artesian spring within, gushing fountains of endless life.'** [43]

'I am the Bread of Life. The person who aligns with me hungers no more and thirsts no more, ever.' [44]

There have been times in my journey with God that were so full of joy, inspiration and spiritual satisfaction that nothing else could ever compare. I can relate to this story from Mike Frost:

'I knew this not just with my mind, but in my body, with my spirit, in my being: that God desired me, wanted me and was demanding that I be His... All I recall is that in the very depths of my soul I sensed God's unrelenting love and acceptance and that this invaded my sexuality, my spirituality, my intellectual and emotional being, my everything, my all... I wept like there was no tomorrow. It was one of the most remarkably healing experiences of my life. I was overwhelmed by God's grace, by His sheer, unadulterated love for me.' [45]

Mick Jagger, the ancient rocker from 70's band The Rolling Stones, has been singing along to their famous guitar lick for years:

> ***I can't get no satisfaction***
> ***I can't get no satisfaction***
> ***'Cause I try, and I try, and I try, and I try***
> ***I can't get no, I can't get no'*** [46]

People can spend their lives using relationships and experiences to feel full and satisfied. Casual sex might feel good in the moment but without lifelong, loving commitment you are soon drifting alone again, leaving pieces of yourself behind. Underneath that desire for sex is a deeper longing: the desire to be truly loved, valued, useful, strong, included and connected.

Take your sexual desire on a drive down a spiritual laneway. Becoming spiritual is not turning off the sexual part of ourselves. It's about putting sex back where it belongs and finding what truly satisfies.

Plug yourself into the truly satisfying power.

You do not just have physical parents; you are a child of God. Before you were born, you were known and loved. You are not an accident.

You are created in God's image. All your bits were put together in great detail through God's creative power. Your choices are real and make your life what it will be. You were made for a purpose; you have important work to do. You can do good in this world. Even when you die, it will not be the end. In Jesus it is only a beginning.

This is God's awesome invitation to you
'Come, all you who are thirsty, come to the waters; and you who have no money, come, buy and eat! Come, buy wine and milk without money and without cost. Why spend money on what is not bread, and your labour on what does not satisfy? Listen, listen to me, and eat what is good, and you will delight in the richest of fare. Give ear and come to me; listen, that you may live.' [47]

Knowing God's real and unending love truly satisfies.

THE LOVE TANK

This is a story about keeping that full feeling.

The GOOD STUFF is people who care, give us attention and bring kindness, understanding, stability, hugs, encouragement and fun into our lives. We all need some good stuff in the tank to survive. On a full tank we thrive.

Some of us have plenty of the good stuff. Some of us have missed out.

Love and friendship are about sharing our supply of the good stuff with people we are close to and trust. The ideal is that we all have a supply to give and share. This makes life good.

Sometimes there isn't a good balance. Sometimes we give more than we should and we start feeling exhausted and empty. Other times, we try to take more than others can give because we need it so badly. Human love is limited, finite. We get tired, we run dry, we don't have enough. When sadness, grief, loneliness and problems come they can leave us feeling empty, thirsty. It can feel like we have nothing to give and no one wants to share their good stuff with us.

We still need SOMETHING in the tank to survive. So we try to fill up on shopping, gaming, sex, internet content, sport, study, work, popularity, fandom, beauty treatments, junk food, adventures, money.

But deep down there is still a thirst.

Long ago, Jeremiah said people are using faulty, smelly bathrooms to find a drink when God is the real living water that truly satisfies.[48]

Jesus once met a woman who had tried many relationships to fill the emptiness. Jesus offered her something much more: a deeper life, a spiritual life.[49]

We were designed to be filled. Connecting to God, we find a supply of the good stuff that never runs out, never runs dry. A never-ending supply that comes from God and can flow into us and out from us to others.[50]

'GOD'S LOVE HAS BEEN POURED OUT INTO OUR HEARTS THROUGH THE HOLY SPIRIT.'[50]

Oh no, You never let go
Through the calm and through the storm
Oh no, You never let go
In every high and every low
Oh no, You never let go
Lord, You never let go of me'[51]

JUDGE NOT

Somehow God's good rules around sex have been put into a special category of 'worst sin ever'. Sadly, some Christians have made people feel that anyone who fails to keep all the laws around sex perfectly don't belong, and when people break the rules it's seen as catastrophe and doom.

Jesus was not like that. Jesus accepted people and hung out with them just as they were. He didn't look down on or reject people because of their behaviour or choices. Jesus was criticised by prideful, cold-hearted religious people for being 'a friend of sinners'. [52]

Follow Jesus' example. Our churches should be places where everyone can come as they are, be honest and find kindness and understanding. Rejecting and judging others is not Jesus' way. Jesus said, 'Do not judge!'

THIS BOOK IS ABOUT THE CHOICES WE MAKE FOR OURSELVES. IT'S NOT A WEAPON TO ACCUSE OR JUDGE ANYBODY ELSE.

Choosing limits on how we use sex is an expression of personal choice. For Christians, our choices are informed by our desire to follow Jesus. Our big mistake is when we try to make everyone else behave the right way rather than putting our energy into making our own behaviour and choices better.

In the book of Romans in the Bible, Paul talks about how human beings ignore God's plan for sex, make up their own rules and are condemned for it, but just after this he writes: 'You, therefore, have no excuse, you who pass judgment on someone else, for at whatever point you judge another, you are condemning yourself, because you who pass judgment do the same things.' [53]

Jesus says something very similar: 'How can you say... "Let me take the speck of dust out of your eye," when all the time there is a plank in your own eye? You hypocrite.' [54]

Every human being is far from perfect. This includes you! Our choices around sex are only one of the ways we fall way short of how God wants us to live. Not sharing our money and possessions, using words to wound people, causing fights and breaking friendships, taking what's not yours, not showing kindness and respect, or just thinking about yourself all the time. These are all things God hates, even while His heart is full of love for you.

It is not the end when people make mistakes or different choices. God made rules about sex so that it can be enjoyed in the right time and place, so that our lives are better not worse. Thinking about what everyone else should be doing – and telling them, thinking you have all the answers, and trying to fix people are all super unhelpful. The best way to help anyone is through kindness and open friendship; through listening, caring and trying to understand.

Think about this: we all have different life experiences. Some of us have had loads of support and care in our lives. Some of us have had big life challenges or felt alone, or perhaps have been hurt by selfish people. The choices that you find easy may not have been easy or even possible for someone else.

Don't judge!

SOLO

It's okay to find pleasure and relief from touching your own body. God loves you, and your body and all its feelings are God's gift to you.

Remember God can help us find wisdom and balance in this space. If you are having a lot of solo sex, it's good to find some other healthy ways to relieve sexual tension. Run, work out, do more sport or even just take a long walk.

Be aware of what you are thinking about when you are touching yourself in a sexual way.

Are you undressing someone in your mind that is not yours to undress?

Are you creating a situation where you have all the power and control? Are you alone or is our good God with you in this place?

Are your thoughts kind, caring and generous? Are you imagining a possible future with a person you will share your whole life with? [55]

'All pornography is centred on the power one has to compel another to do as you demand; therefore, it is about control, dominance and ultimately degradation. All masturbation that finds its core image centred on power, use and degradation violates true self-pleasure.

It makes the heart small and cheap.

On the other hand, masturbation that imagines the man or woman who by character, generosity, and love – let alone beauty and desire – arouses you is meant to stir the body and heart to pleasure. The warning is not to let the flame consume the boundaries of honour and care before one is ready.' [56"]

'"I have the right to do anything," you say – but not everything is beneficial. "I have the right to do anything" – but I will not be mastered by anything.' [57]

WARNING!

DO NOT MIX WITH PORNOGRAPHY

Interferes with natural arousal

Creates unreal expectations and kills the joyful discovery of a real person and their natural body at the right time

Promotes the growth of selfish and controlling behaviour

May cause chronic long-term relational health problems

Can result in serious addiction

Reduces the heartbeat of true love

SPECTATOR SPORT

Chances are you will see people having sex on screen. It's hard to avoid, often in the shows we like to watch. Have you ever noticed the way this watching can make you feel?

Pornography is images and video of people having sex. Watching porn can create strong overwhelming feelings of sexual desire in your body even before your brain has registered. It makes you feel an intensity you were never meant to feel on your own away from real life.

Watching porn is like flying close to a black hole. It can be addictive like drugs. The attraction centre in your brain goes on producing intense cravings to look at more, and more... and more. [58]

Sex was never meant to be watched. It was designed to be felt and experienced by two people in a secret loving place, expressing their heartfelt, lifelong commitment to each other, far, far away from any camera or spying eyes.

Porn is not like real-life sex. It makes it harder for you to enjoy sex in the awesome way God intended. Real-life lovemaking is about learning to think of the other person and not yourself; porn puts you in a selfish frame of mind. In real life you have to be vulnerable. The other person gets to see your body, it's not a one-way experience you can turn on and off when you like. Also, in reality, people do not have sex on demand. They have good days and bad days, they get sick, tired and busy. Sometimes they want sex and sometimes they really don't. The loving thing to do is wait or go without.

In real life it's not all about you.

PORN	REAL-LIFE, HEALTHY RELATIONSHIPS
Just bodies	Whole people, connecting bodies, minds, emotions and lives
Illusion of a perfect body, impossible standards and totally unreal expectations	True beauty is real people (including yourself) with bumps, scars, flabby bits and natural hair
A person's body is a thing to be stared at, used, bought and sold	Two people can give the gift of their bodies to each other when it's the right time
No consideration of feelings	Empathy, understanding and care for how others feel is the only way to build a real relationship
2D and alone	3D and together, all five senses and more
On demand when I want it	Requires patience and communication
Focussed on me – my pleasure, my feelings	About us – sharing pleasure, feelings and the whole of life together

BE A REBEL. TAKE BACK THE POWER FROM A PROFIT-DRIVEN, GLOBAL, FAKE SEX INDUSTRY ALSO INVOLVED IN HUMAN SLAVERY AND CHILD ABUSE. [59]

HOW TO AVOID PORN

- *Close your eyes.*
- *Close the device and don't look for it again. Delete any texts or links that connected you.*
- *Put your brain into action. Name it and shame it:*
    - *This isn't cool – ditch it!*
    - *That is ugly – I don't want to see it!*
    - *That is not how sex is supposed to be!*
- *You might have a lot of sexual feelings or energy inside. Get active. Run or walk a few k's, smash a few balls or work out.*
- *Do something fun and healthy instead – talk with friends, get fit, solve a complex problem, help someone in need, write a song or your first novel, learn skateboarding, plant a tree or raise money for charity.*
- *Talk about what you have seen with someone wiser and older – your parents or someone else trustworthy.*

WATCHING SPORT FOR HOURS DOES NOTHING TO GET YOU READY FOR YOUR REAL-LIFE MATCH DAY.

If you have seen porn, don't suggest copying what you have seen. If you do ever get to experience sex with a lifelong lover it will be so much better just to figure it out together. You'll make a few mistakes, and maybe even have a few laughs, as you work out how to give each other awesome pleasure. You might need a bit of wise or technical advice along the way, but you really can do without manufactured, fake images invading your head in that special real-life moment.

If you can't stop watching porn, even if you want to, you may have an addiction. Don't let the black hole suck you in. It's embarrassing and you probably want to hide it, but it's really important to tell someone, maybe one of your parents or another trustworthy adult. There are people who can help you get into a healthier head space. [60]

A Word from TJ

In a YouTube interview, Brittni De La Mora asked her pastor this question:

'WHAT WOULD YOU DO IF YOU FOUND ONE OF YOUR KIDS WATCHING PORNOGRAPHY?'

Pastor TJ's answer is thoughtful, kind and understanding. Just the kind of thing we'd like to hear from our parents or tell our own kids one day.

'First of all, I would shut off the computer and take the laptop. I would say, "Hey, we are going to talk about this. We don't have to talk about it right now but let's do it over some food. Italian or tacos? Which would you like?" He's probably feeling scared to death at this point but I don't want to shame him, I want to empower him.

'So I'm gonna take my son out for tacos or whatever he chooses. I'm going to affirm our relationship and tell him he is the best son I ever had. I will tell him that he is a gift from God to me and that no matter what he does in this life he will never disqualify himself from being loved by me.

'I want to let him know that at some level I can understand. Watching porn is not good, but normal.

I'll tell him I remember being his age. "You may not believe it, but I remember how hard it is to manage those emotions and feelings with all these beautiful women. It's hard to know what is what."

'I'll say, "You are going to have such a great future" and remind him of who he is and that porn is not a thing that aligns with who he is and the good future he has ahead of him.'

The way I was brought up, my parents' response would have been much more shaming. They would have said, 'Don't you do that! If I ever catch you again you will be in trouble.' This just drags you into more secrecy and shame.

TJ continues: 'I think of lust and all of those things like water boiling in a pan. A lot of the time we put a lid on it. But as it gets hotter, it ends up boiling over. You never really fix a problem by putting a lid on it. Problems are solved by opening up and being honest about it. You would be surprised if you sit around with people; there are a lot of people that are struggling with issues just like you. We are all trying to figure it out.

'I want you to know that the way to heal from this is not for you to just go fix it on your own. We heal through community, we heal through understanding God's love for us.

If you would become vulnerable and open up, you will find healing you have never experienced before. Open up, let somebody know. You are not abnormal, you are not weird, you are human. God is divine. He loves you and you are going to make it.' [61]

YOUNG PEOPLE DON'T NEED SHAME. THEY NEED LOVING, KIND AND ENCOURAGING RELATIONSHIPS AND A VISION FOR THE FUTURE.

SAME-SEX SEX

Some people feel sexual and romantic attraction to people of the same sex. These feelings of attraction can be strong for a certain stage in life and then change over time; for others it's an experience of life that's always there and doesn't change.

Churches and Christians have often found it difficult to understand and care for people with same-sex attraction. They have been so concerned about keeping rules, they have not shown anywhere near enough kindness. People are not rejected by God, unloved or bad because they feel same-sex attraction. If this is you, please remember the opening message of this book:

What many people think now about romantic and sexual relationships between people of the same-sex is different to what Christians have accepted over the last two thousand years. Marriage between same-sex couples is legal in many countries and people would say that sex, romance and having a partner are so important in life that it would be unfair and unkind to ask anyone to live without having them.

Christians don't all see same-sex relationships the same way. What makes us Christian is our relationship to Jesus, not our view of same-sex relationships but it is an important issue to think through. Recent writers have used 'Side A and Side B' to describe the different views of people who read the Bible and are seeking to follow Jesus. [62-64]. It's always good to see people with different views having kind, honest and respectful conversations with each other.

This is a good place to pause and review the story of this book so far…

THE STORY SO FAR...

- Sex is not a cure for the real spiritual hunger that is the source of our desires.

- Sex was never meant to be the ultimate meaning of life. Our sexual attractions do not help us find out who we really are or move us towards ultimate meaning and fulfilment. Having sex is not necessary to be a fully alive, happy, functioning and flourishing human being. There is a whole load of life to live and enjoy apart from sex.

- Sexuality is a flow of powerful feelings, energy and vitality within each of us. Sex can bring great pleasure and joy to life but it can also bring great pain and many troubles. Sexual attraction by itself is not a good way to decide what is best to do.

- True satisfaction is found in God. Our identity and worth is not in being attractive, having an active sex life or even having children. Our life purpose is connection to God and bringing God's love and truth and wisdom into the world.

- Sex was not designed to be a casual sport or a way of passing time. It was God's idea to bring and hold two very different human beings together for life. It was designed as a gift to bond those who have agreed to lifelong faithfulness to each other and are open to welcoming children.

- Our world is a confusing place when it comes to sex. The Bible talks about how we have all gone off track from God's original intentions. This has affected every human being and nature too. Not all the things we want to do are good or best for us.

MORE TO SAY

For followers of Jesus, the Bible can't just be ignored or discounted. It's our complicated but vitally important ancient guidebook. Challenging and sometimes difficult, the Bible is also full of inspiration and beauty. A text three thousand years in the making, it's a gift that holds the deepest wisdom about the all-wise, all-loving, creative, kind, faithful, just and true God. It's also a guide for how best to live our lives.

- The Bible says that the lifelong, committed relationship between a man and a woman is unique. God designed human beings with male and female body parts. It's important for Christians to respect God's original physical design and purpose for sex. [65]
- The Bible doesn't approve sexual activity between people of the same physical sex. [66]
- The purpose of sex includes the natural possibility of babies being made and new families being created, where children can find loving connection with a mother and a father.
- There are health implications of certain sexual practices that go beyond God's design and the natural use of our bodies. [67]
- Marriage was not designed for everyone. Jesus, the most loving, kind and wise human ever, was single. Same-sex attracted followers of Jesus can follow Jesus' beautiful example into kind, close and faithful friendships without sexual activity and find freedom to live in God, share His love and bless the world. [68]
- When Christians have different views, or see the Bible in a different way, we need to follow the example of Jesus and care for each other; being prepared to listen and share with kindness and respect.

'YOU ARE NOT YOUR OWN; YOU WERE BOUGHT AT A PRICE. THEREFORE HONOUR GOD WITH YOUR BODIES.' [69]

DAVID

'As a nineteen-year-old gay activist who felt rejected by Christianity, I had very little reason to believe in God,' says David Bennett. 'Then I encountered Jesus in a pub in the gay quarter of Sydney, Australia and my life changed forever.' [70]

In David's book, A War of Loves, he talks about being gay as part of his personal reality. He still dated guys after he became a Christian, but after a few years wrestling with God and honestly searching, he sees the Bible's teaching on sex as reasonably clear. He has chosen to be celibate and not have an active sex life. He writes, 'I have chosen, by God's grace, to give my sexuality to Jesus Christ.' [Fn 71]

This might seem unfair, or limiting or sad, but David doesn't see it that way. He says that people today are obsessed with romantic love and wrongly believe you can't have your best life without sex.

'I am actually grateful for being gay or same-sex attracted, because it means I can no longer worship the gods of our culture... I was told for so long that my sexual desires were what defined my humanity. But as a Christian, I learned that giving ourselves to God completely and trusting him with our same-sex desires is precious in his eyes. It helps us see that he is our greatest treasure and what we are really longing for. The goal of our lives isn't to fulfil our culture's expectations and worship our own desires but to follow Jesus and worship God. I have given up a portion of myself but in return, I found my whole humanity.' [72]

JACKIE

Jackie Hill Perry (who we will meet again shortly) grew up being same-sex attracted. As a young adult her girlfriend was a huge part of her life. One day Jackie was surprised by a deep experience of God's presence and power. She chose to leave her same-sex relationship behind.

'God was not calling me to be straight; He was calling me to himself...God was not a Las Vegas chaplain or an impatient mother intent on sending a man my way to 'cure' my homosexuality. He was God. A God after my whole heart, desperate to make it new. Committed to making it like Him. In my becoming holy as He is, I would not be miraculously made into a woman that didn't like women; I'd be made into a woman that loved God more than anything. If marriage ever came or singleness called my name, He wanted to guarantee by the work of His hands that both would be lived unto him'. [73]

PINK-BOY, BLUE-GIRL

In the observation of day-to-day life we see differences between men and women, boys and girls. One important difference is that people either have a male or a female body. Some extremely rare and unique people are a physical blend of both biological sexes. [76]

Apart from the body, what's the difference between the sexes?

No matter what qualities are on this list, it's impossible to not tick both boxes for both sexes. Think of the countries and cultures in the world and different times in history. There are many versions of what was thought to be 'for women' or 'for men'. Men in eighteenth-century England wore curly wigs and colourful, lacy clothing, and in the Pacific Islands men feel very comfortable wearing skirts. The Samsui women of Singapore did backbreaking labour on construction sites and women now lift weights and enjoy contact sports. Also, there are always exceptional people, unique people who just don't fit the general mould for their biological sex.

At best, we can only say the non-biological differences are 'subtle'. Apart from being spelled in a really weird way, 'subtle', according to a quick Google search, means differences that are 'so delicate or precise as to be difficult to analyse or describe'.

SUBTLE IS GOOD. AVOID RULES THAT PUT PEOPLE IN BOXES.

	Men and boys	Women and girls
Like sport	✓	✓
Like dressing up	✓	✓
Play to win	✓	✓
Play for fun	✓	✓
Are physically strong and active	✓	✓
Have deep thoughts and feelings	✓	✓
Good at maths and science	✓	✓
Enjoy literature and art	✓	✓
Attracted to physical appearance	✓	✓
Attracted to personality	✓	✓
Blue, plain	✓	✓
Pink, floral	✓	✓
Wear pants	✓	✓
Wear skirts	✓	✓
Competitive and decisive	✓	✓
Caring and thoughtful	✓	✓
Excellent dancers and musicians	✓	✓
Clear-thinking and decisive leaders	✓	✓
Calm and quiet	✓	✓
Noisy and loud	✓	✓
Talk about practical and technical things	✓	✓
Talk about feelings and relationships	✓	✓
Like fashion and beauty treatments	✓	✓
Like dressing to be comfortable	✓	✓
Can paint, draw, create, perform	✓	✓
Can make and fix stuff	✓	✓

COMFORT AND BALANCE

'We can say one thing with a high degree of confidence – something that's not widely disputed: whatever differences might exist between "male brains" and "female brains," these differences are based on generalities not absolutes.' [77]

'That is for boys.' 'This is for girls.' 'You belong, you don't belong.' 'You act the right way, you don't.' Part of growing up is leaving this kind of thinking behind. Your particular likes, activity preferences, strengths, weaknesses and personality might be in the majority or the minority of your biological sex, but these things don't make you any less male or female,' [78]

You might be a short male person who is a talented dancer or musician, or a tall female person who is a gifted scientist or mathematician. You might be a male or a female person who likes working on engines, or loves cooking meals for friends and looking after children.

LET'S AVOID EXTREMES AND FIND BALANCE, BE LESS ONE SIDE OR ANOTHER.

In the book of Genesis we read that God created human beings IN HIS IMAGE. This means that God and his human reflection Jesus are 'the model of the most exquisitely integrated being'. 'The Christian idea of God provides us with the template we require in the work of being healthy sexual beings.' [79]

God has ALL the awesome traits that we might associate with the two sexes. God is clear-sighted, logical, creative, caring, powerful, full of love and so much more. Jesus in a human form shows us what God is like. Jesus was powerful and peaceful. He expressed anger and tears, He was focussed on big picture goals as well as expressing great kindness and empathy.

The Bible tells stories of active and courageous men and women, like David, Jael, Esther and Stephen, as well as thoughtful and compassionate men and women, like Mary, Solomon, John and Tabitha. [80]

According to the Bible, having male and female people was part of God's very good plan. This means there must be ways to enjoy the subtle differences between men and women without unhelpful rigid rules. When the differences between the sexes are loud we need to turn down the volume, but we would probably miss something interesting and beautiful if we never heard the music of those subtle differences.

Life can be really challenging and confusing for people who feel disconnected or uncomfortable with their biological sex. Some people say they experience a sense of self that doesn't seem to match their physical body and they may change their body or the way they look to try and feel more at ease. Life can be so confusing but kindness, acceptance and seeking to love and understand is the best way to help anyone.

If you are less typical of your biological sex you can actually help us all with this. If you can be brave enough to be yourself, express your own personality and preferences, you will be a great example and help others be less rigid and fixed in their ideas of who they are or are expected to be.

Jackie Hill Perry is a writer, poet and artist. In her book *Gay Girl, Good God*, Jackie describes how she grew up feeling uncomfortable, not fitting the mould of what people thought a woman should be. When Jackie got to know God she found strength and peace in knowing that God was with her just as she was; other people's opinions didn't matter anymore.

'I wasn't considered girly enough for the world. When age took hold, I distanced myself from what some considered feminine. Pink was ugly, so I didn't wear it. Dresses were awkward, so I didn't put them on. Purses were inconvenient so I didn't hold them. These things were to them what made girls, girls… society called me manly. They'd made women out to be people who wear their legs out and men to be those that spoke as if everyone should listen. Neither version were a sufficient mirror. I'd need someone smarter and not created to tell me who I was, for He would be the one who'd known best…

The body I lived in felt like I'd been given the wrong clothing. Another shirt looked better, warmer, easier to put on. Mine, stranger, uncomfortable, itchy and impossible to take off.

If I were able to see God's goodness in all that He'd made, including me and my woman-ness, then I would have easily understood that my body was not left out from the words of Colossians 1:16: "For by him all things were created, in heaven and on earth, visible and invisible… all things were created through Him and for him".

My hands, head, face, legs, hips, hormones, private parts, voice, feet, fingers, feelings, were all made by Him and for Him; apparently this body was never mine to begin with – it was given to me from Somebody, for Somebody. Somebody who'd made it for glory and not for shame.' [81]

ALTERATIONS

'IT'S THE BRAVE [PERSON] WHO SAYS, "I DON'T CARE WHAT ANYONE THINKS, I AM HAPPY IN MY OWN SKIN."' [82]

'We can compare ourselves to everyone else or begin to understand that sunsets, oceans, flowers and rainforests, even though they are all intensely beautiful, look nothing alike.' [83]

'I've been in a wheelchair my whole life. I was born with a tumour wrapped around my spinal cord that was cut out when I was only a couple of days old... I've known nothing but having a disability, and if I'm honest with you, I can't tell you how much I used to hate myself. I used to hate having a disability. I hated it so much, I hated being different and I didn't want to be here anymore. I really didn't. I believed that was going to be my life... I sit here as a proud man with a disability tonight. I love my disability. It is the best thing that ever happened to me. It really is, and I'm so thankful for the life that I get to live... I love the person that I am and the life I get to live.' [84]

'It feels like societal brainwashing. The idea that you must be fixed because you are not beautiful enough the way you naturally are... I don't think women should be brainwashed from the age of 13 to think that they are only gorgeous if they look like, you know, not themselves... Trying to look like Kylie Jenner for the rest of your life is just going to make you sad.' [85]

'I actually look at my younger self and think why did I pound myself with make up? I actually made myself look worse. I was so heavily invested in my appearance at such a young age. I should have been focusing on... making memories with my friends. If I had a child one day I hope she doesn't feel the need to change herself physically in order to be beautiful, to feel accepted and loved.' [86]

It's an awesome feeling to be comfortable, to feel content with how you look, to be at peace with your natural body, to just enjoy being yourself. But there's this pressure...

A thousand images, advertisers and influencers eating away at us, undercutting our physical confidence. So many people feel really sensitive about how they look. It's hard to resist feeling wrong, ugly and insecure. And then there are the companies that sell beauty products and provide cosmetic enhancement procedures. They make loads of money convincing us that we need to change our appearance to get rid of the crushing anxiety and find a confident sense of self.

It's good to take some time to look your best, enjoy the fun and individuality of fashion, dress for a fancy party and wear great make up. It feels good to work out, get fitter and stronger, have a cool haircut. There are reasons why a visit to a beauty therapist or plastic surgeon might be helpful, and everyone likes it when we wash and wear deodorant but:

'I think we would all be happier and have a more satisfied life if we didn't feel the need to change ourselves all the time.' [87]

People can now spend loads of money, time and energy trying to create the body and the look they desire for themselves. But true beauty and peace cannot be found via a daily workout, diet, a surgeon's knife or needle injection. Maybe all that money, time and energy could be spent on things that will really last instead of on a look that is only skin deep that will fade and die.

'Therefore I tell you, do not worry about your life, what you will eat or drink; or about your body; what you will wear. Is not life more than food, and the body more than clothes?' [88]

'The Lord does not look at the things people look at. People look at the outward appearance, but the Lord looks at the heart.' [89]

Truly beautiful people see below the skin in themselves and others. They are interested in people's thoughts and values, whether they are generous, welcoming or self-focussed, uncaring and mean.

Jesus never ever judged by outward appearance. He saw right through physical appearance into people's hearts and inner lives. Jesus saw the light or darkness, kindness or selfishness, peace or chaos that was inside. Jesus valued true beauty and through Jesus we find peace.

CONSUMER OR COVENANT?

We can treat sex like shopping: you check out all your options, swipe right, swipe left; it's just a transaction like buying and selling. As long as it's fair, equal, legal, consensual everybody can get what they want. Buy, sell, swap, transaction complete.

'A CORD OF THREE STRANDS IS NOT QUICKLY BROKEN.'[90]

For followers of Jesus, sex is not a shopping trip. It's a covenant. Deeper and far more valuable than anything we can buy, it expresses without words your support, your choice, your commitment and promise to be on the same team forever. It says WE not I. The team of two together; three including God.

'Thinkers have long discerned the difference between a consumer relationship which is characterized by the marketplace, and a covenantal relationship... A consumer relationship is maintained only as long as the consumer gets goods and services at an acceptable price. There is no obligation for the consumer to stay in the relationship if it is not profitable... a covenantal relationship is based not on favourable conditions of value but on a loving commitment to the good of the other person and to the relationship itself... Traditionally, you did not have sex with someone that was not your spouse. Put another way, you didn't give your body to someone unless you committed your whole life to them (and they to you) and you both gave up your individual freedom to bind yourself in the covenant of marriage. Contemporary adults want freedom, including sexual freedom. So they have sex with each other without committing their lives to one another, which typically leads to chronic loneliness and a sense of being used – and well it should. Sex in our culture is no longer something that unites people together in a binding community; it is a commodity for exchange. But the Bible tells us that sex is designed by God, not as a means of self-gratification, but as a means of self-donation that creates stable human community.' [91]

THE BIG, BEAUTIFUL PROMISES FOR A WEDDING DAY

Will you give yourself?
Will you live with this person according to God's word?
Will you love, comfort, honour and protect?
And, forsaking all others, be faithful as long as you both shall live?
Will you say YES?

*In the presence of God,
I take you,
To have and to hold from this day forward,
For better, for worse,
For richer, for poorer,
In sickness and in health, to love and to cherish,
So long as we both shall live.
All this I vow and promise.* [92]

These four hundred-year-old words describe Christian marriage as a big, beautiful promise. A covenant with a lifelong, rain, hail or shine intention. Its more than a beautiful day to celebrate the love of two people.

MARRIAGE IS A PICTURE OF SOMETHING EVEN DEEPER AND GREATER. IT HELPS US UNDERSTAND HOW GOD WANTS TO BE CONNECTED TO EVERY SINGLE ONE OF US.

The word covenant also describes God's promises. They are like the promises people make when they marry, but even stronger because, unlike human beings, God always keeps His promises, His covenant.

GOD SAYS, 'I'LL NEVER LET YOU DOWN, NEVER WALK OFF AND LEAVE YOU.' [93]

FOLLOWING

FOLLOWING ME

> I'll work out what's best for me. It's my life. Rules aren't important. I'll choose what is best and I'll follow advice that I think will work for me.
>
> If I make the wrong choice, life could go wrong; I might miss out or mess up but hopefully I'll enjoy being alive and everything will work out.
>
> *People make their own value.*

FOLLOWING RULES

> I must work really hard to obey God so that bad things won't happen to me. God's rules should never be broken.
>
> When I'm doing well, I can feel proud of myself, because I'm better than other people. I don't want to fail because then I would be a bad person. I wouldn't be loved.
>
> *People are only valuable when they do what's right.*

FOLLOWING JESUS

> **I am truly and eternally loved by God. Because of this real love and because God knows what is best for me, I choose to follow God's way. I am not perfect, so I can't look down on others. I make mistakes and wrong choices but it's not the end; God forgives. I am always valuable and loved because God's love never ends.**
>
> **God's constant love is not something you need a credit card to pay for. It's not dependent on perfect life choices or earned by being good. God's love costs us nothing but Jesus, the perfect example of God's love, God gave everything; His whole life, so that we could know and live in unending love.**
>
> *People are always valuable and loved.*

A LAST WORD

> Trust GOD from the bottom of your heart;
>   don't try to figure out everything on your own.
> Listen for GOD's voice in everything you do, everywhere you go;
>   he's the one who will keep you on track.
> Don't assume that you know it all.
>   Run to GOD! Run from evil!
> Your body will glow with health,
>   your very bones will vibrate with life! [95]

READ, WATCH, LISTEN

We all need help and advice sometimes.

It can be challenging and hard to find the words, but the most helpful thing to do if you have questions, worries and concerns about anything to do with sex, relationships and gender is talk. Look for a a trusted, caring and wise parent, friend, teacher or Christian leader. If you need more; sessions with a psychologist or counsellor can help too. It might take a few tries to find someone you feel safe and comfortable working with. Sharing what's really going on for you is the best way to make a positive change.

BOOKS

Sam Allberry, Is God Anti-gay? (Surrey, UK: The Good Book Company, 2013)

Dan Allender and Tremper Longman, God Loves Sex (Grand Rapids, MI: Baker Books, 2014)

David Bennett, A War of Loves (Grand Rapids, MI: Zondervan, 2018)

Mike Frost, Longing for Love (Australia & New Zealand: Albatross Books, 1996)

Ed Shaw, The Plausibility Problem (Nottingham, UK: IVP, 2015)

Preston Sprinkle, People to Be Loved (Grand Rapids, MI: Zondervan, 2015)

Preston Sprinkle, Embodied (Colorado Springs, CO: David C Cook, 2021)

Patricia Weerakoon, Teen Sex by the Book (Sydney South: Anglican Youthworks, 2019)

WORLD WIDE WEB

bigkidstable – follow on Instagram, Tiktok or Facebook

christian-sexuality.com/videos

collectiveshout.org – *a movement against the objectification of women and the sexualisation of girls*

fightthenewdrug.org – *information about the effects of porn using only science, facts and personal accounts*

joinfortify.com – *tools for individuals struggling with compulsive pornography use*

livingout.org – *helping people, churches and society talk about faith and sexuality*

www.tiktok.com/@brittnidelamora – *Brittni has an incredible story*

xxxchurch.com/blog – *insight, advice and encouragement from a community of writers on the topics of porn addiction and sexual integrity*

eXXXamine series on YouTube – *real conversations about porn and purity*

PODCASTS

Search and subscribe on your favourite podcast app.

- All Strings Attached with Angela Blair
- Theology in the Raw with Preston Sprinkle
- Unbelievable? with Justin Brierly
- Undeceptions with John Dickson

FOR PARENTS, CARERS AND YOUTH LEADERS

bigkidstable.org – *bringing an informative, loving perspective and creating safe, honest conversations about kingdom identity, sexual experience and the expression of sexual desire for youth and young adults of faith*

christian-sexuality.com – *resources to help Christian youth and young adults follow Jesus with their sexuality*

educateempowerkids.org – *teaching about digital citizenship, media literacy and healthy sexuality, including education about the dangers of online pornography*

centerforfaith.com – *The Center for Faith, Sexuality & Gender is a collaboration of Christian pastors, leaders and theologians who aspire to be the church's most trusted source of theologically sound teaching and practical guidance on questions related to sexuality and gender*

NOTES

Chapter 1 You Are Loved
1 Romans 8:38–9, The Message.

Chapter 2 Body Balance
2 Psalm 139:13–4.
3 Genesis 1:27, 31, NRSV.
4 1 Corinthians 12:18.
5 Matthew 10:30.

Chapter 3 The Book in the Middle
6 Song of Songs 1:2,4; 1:13, 15–6; 4:11; 3:4; 4:16b–5:1; 8:2–3. (The Song of Songs is also called the Song of Solomon.)
7 Dan Allender and Tremper Longman, God Loves Sex (Grand Rapids, MI: Baker Books, 2014), 139.
8 Song of Songs 8:6–7, NRSV.
9 Song of Songs 2:7; 3:5; 8:4.
10 God Loves Sex, 139.

Chapter 4 Swimming
11 https://www.smh.com.au/national/picnic-drowning-shatters-a-family-20041227-gdkdyh.html
12 Mark 10:5–9, The Message.
13 1 Corinthians 6:16–7, The Message.

Chapter 5 Cake
14 Jonathan Franzen, Purity (London: 4th Estate, 2016).
15 Judy Douglas.
16 Alex Lee.

Chapter 6 Powerful
17 Andrew Wilson, The True Sexual Revolution, https://www.livingout.org/resources/articles/10/the-true-sexual-revolution
18 Patricia Weerakoon, Teen Sex by the Book (Sydney South: Anglican Youthworks, 2019) and
Dawn Maslar, 'The Love Biologist', Episode 1, 22 May 2022, in All Strings Attached podcast presented by Angela Blair. Watch Dawn Maslar describe her research on this Ted X talk: https://youtu.be/eyq2Wo4eUDg

Chapter 7 Verb
19 Luke 6:27.
20 John Green, 'Indianapolis and Love at First Sight', Episode 12, 31 January 2019, in The Anthropocene Reviewed podcast.
21 1 Corinthians 13:4–8, with help from various translations.
22 'Real Love', track 8 on Tex Perkins, Far Be It From Me, Polydor Records Australia, 1996.

Chapter 8 Controller
23 Philippians 2:3–4, ICB.
24 Clifford Penner & Joyce Penner, Getting Your Sex Life Off to a Great Start (Nashville, TN: Thomas Nelson), 138–9.

Chapter 9 Entrée or Main?
25 'We feel it foolish to think that outside of marriage there should be no physical intimacy between a man and a woman. In answer to how far is too far, we have heard those who teach that even kissing and intimate touching should be reserved for marriage. Such a view is unrealistic and even absurd and puts unbelievable pressures on young single people, particularly in modern times when marriage tends to be delayed till long after the point of sexual maturation. Perhaps the best principle, though it is not a law, it that the level of intimacy should not exceed the level of commitment that a man and a woman have for each other. A couple that is engaged have entered a level of commitment that is far beyond that of a couple in their first month of dating, but still short of the full-blown commitment of marriage. Physical intimacy should not exceed the level of commitment that a couple have for each other.' God Loves Sex, 119–20.
26 God Loves Sex, 121.

Chapter 10 The Sex Myth
27 Rachel Hills, The Sex Myth (Penguin Random House Australia, 2015).
28 The Sex Myth, 8, 35.
29 The Sex Myth, 2.
30 'Closer', track 5 on Nine Inch Nails, The Downward Spiral, Island Records, 1994.
31 'Take Me to Church', track 1 on Hozier, Hozier, Island Records, 2014.
32 'Meaning of Life', track 4 on Kelly Clarkson, Meaning of Life, Atlantic Records, 2017.
33 C. S. Lewis, The Weight of Glory. Preached originally as a sermon in the Church of St Mary the Virgin, Oxford, 8 June 1942, published in Theology, November 1941, and by SPCK, 1942, https://www.wheelersburg.net/Downloads/Lewis%20Glory.pdf

Chapter 11 Monk Life
34 For example, Mary, Martha and Lazarus. See John 11:1–3, 36.
35 1 Corinthians 7:7, The Message.
36 1 Corinthians 7:32–5.

Chapter 12 Single-minded
37 Mike Frost, Longing for Love (Australia & New Zealand: Albatross Books, 1996), 284.
38 https://www.livingout.org/resources/articles/69/marriage-as-a-trailer
39 Anna McGahan, Metanoia (Sydney: Acorn Press, 2019), 285.
40 Metanoia, 123.

Chapter 13 Satisfied
41 Matthew 5:6, GNT; see Psalm 103:5.
42 'Jesus, Strong and Kind', Colin Buchanan, Jonny Robinson, Michael Farren, Rich Thompson, CityAlight Music, 2019.
43 John 4:13–4, The Message.
44 John 6:35, The Message.
45 Longing for Love, 231–2.
46 '(I Can't Get No) Satisfaction', track 1, side two on The Rolling Stones, Out of Our Heads, London Records, 1965.
47 Isaiah 55:1-3

Chapter 14 The Love Tank
48 Jeremiah 2:13 says, 'My people have committed two sins: They have forsaken me, the spring of living water, and have dug their own cisterns, broken cisterns that cannot hold water.'
49 John 4:7–28.
50 Romans 5:5.
51 'You Never Let Go', track 2 on Matt Redman, Beautiful News, sixstepsrecords, 2006.

Chapter 15 Judge Not
52 See Matthew 11:19; Luke 7:34.
53 Matthew 7:1.
54 Romans 2:1.
55 Matthew 7:4–5.

Chapter 16 Solo
56 God Loves Sex, 139–40.
57 1 Corinthians 6:12.

Chapter 17 Spectator Sport
58 https://fightthenewdrug.org/is-porn-addiction-even-a-real-thing/. The article says that there are now over thirty-five neuroscience-based studies, using a variety of brain-imaging technologies (MRI, fMRI, EEG, etc.), that provide solid support for the reality of internet porn addiction. There are more than forty studies that link compulsive porn use to depression, anxiety and poorer mental health functioning in general.
59 Angela Blair, 'All Strings Attached', Episode 7, February 2022, in The Activist podcast.
60 Online resources that may help: xxxchurch.com; Fightthenewdrug.org; Joinfortify.com

Chapter 18 TJ Says
61 'Ex Porn-star Interviews a Pastor', Brittni De La Mora and Pastor TJ Anglin, https://www.youtube.com/watch?v=AW1vPPgfxgA

Chapter 19 Same-Sex Sex
62 David Bennett, A War of Loves (Grand Rapids, MI: Zondervan, 2018), Chapter 14 and Appendix 1.
63 See Justin Lee, Torn (Jericho Books USA, 2012), 221–5; A War of Loves, 199–200; https://www.youtube.com/watch?v=kMsv6ZBK8SE (Brandan Robertson (Side A) and David Bennett (Side B) in conversation on the podcast Unbelievable?).
64 Justin Lee, Brandan Robertson and Matthew Vines are all Side A Christians. See Torn by Justin Lee, www.brandanrobertson.com and www.matthewvines.com.

Chapter 20 More to Say
65 Tim Keller, Christianity and Homosexuality: A Review of Books, https://www.redeemer.com/redeemer-report/article/christianity_and_homosexuality_a_review_of_books, 2013.
66 Preston Sprinkle, People to Be Loved (Grand Rapids, MI: Zondervan, 2015), Chapter 9 and 187–92.
67 Teen Sex by the Book, 202.
68 Ed Shaw, The Plausibility Problem (Nottingham, UK: IVP, 2015); Wesley Hill, Washed and Waiting (Grand Rapids, MI: Zondervan, 2017); Sam Allberry, Is God Anti-gay? (Surrey, UK: The Good Book Company, 2013).
69 1 Corinthians 6:19–20.
70 A War of Loves, 17.
71 A War of Loves, 19.
72 A War of Loves, 203–4.
73 Jackie Hill Perry, Gay Girl, Good God (Nashville, TN: B&H Publishing, 2018), 69.

Chapter 21 Pink-boy, Blue-girl
76 Preston Sprinkle, Embodied (Colorado Springs, CO: David C Cook, 2021), 122. Also see Preston Sprinkle's longer discussion from 117-123.

Chapter 22 Comfort and Balance
77 Embodied,135.
78 Teen Sex by the Book, 170–1.
79 Longing for Love, 67–8.
80 David: 1 Samuel 17; Jael: Judges 4; Esther: Esther 4 and 5; Stephen: Acts 7; Mary: Luke 2:19; Solomon: 1 Kings 4; John: John 21; Tabitha: Acts 9.
81 Gay Girl, Good God, 48–52.

Chapter 23 Alterations
82 Kirstie Clement, former editor-in-chief of Vogue Australia, 'Empowerment or exploitation?', Episode 4, 22 May 2022, in Face Value podcast presented and produced by Siobhan Marin: RN Presents by ABC Radio Australia.
83 Facebook meme.
84 Dylan Alcott, champion wheelchair tennis athlete and Australian of the Year 2022. Full text of his acceptance speech on 26 January 2022 is at https://www.abc.net.au/news/2022-01-26/dylan-alcott-australian-of-the-year-speech-in-full/100783308
85 Kina, age fourteen, Face Value, Episode 4.
86 Natasha, Face Value, Episode 4.
87 Heather Widdows, Face Value, Episode 4.
88 Matthew 6:25.
89 1 Samuel 16:7.

Chapter 24 Consumer or Covenant?
90 Ecclesiastes 4:12.
91 Tim Keller, Center Church (Grand Rapids, MI: Zondervan, 2012), 128.
92 Anglican Church of Australia Trust Corporation, A Prayer Book for Australia (Mulgrave, Victoria: Broughton Publishing, 2010), 660–1.
93 See Hebrews 13:5; Deuteronomy 31:6.

Chapter 25 Following
94 Center Church, 63–5. With thanks to Tim Keller for the very useful concept of 'three ways to live'

Chapter 26 A Last Word
95 Proverbs 3:5–8, The Message.

www.ingramcontent.com/pod-product-compliance
Lightning Source LLC
Chambersburg PA
CBHW061139010526
44107CB00069B/2985